KNIGHTS IN ARMOR

Shirley Glubok

Designed by Gerard Nook

HARPER & ROW, PUBLISHERS · NEW YORK, EVANSTON, AND LONDON

From Codex Manesse, German, fourteenth century
The University of Heidelberg Library

The author gratefully acknowledges the assistance of
THOMAS T. HOOPES, Curator Emeritus, City Art Museum of St. Louis
HELMUT NICKEL, Associate Curator, Department of Arms and Armor, The Metropolitan Museum of Art
MARGARET R. SCHERER, former Research Associate, The Metropolitan Museum of Art
NICHOLAS and CHARLES DAVIDSON
WILLIAM and LAURENCE WEINBAUM

Other books by Shirley Glubok

THE ART OF ANCIENT EGYPT
THE ART OF LANDS IN THE BIBLE
THE ART OF ANCIENT GREECE
THE ART OF THE NORTH AMERICAN INDIAN
THE ART OF THE ESKIMO
THE ART OF ANCIENT ROME
THE ART OF AFRICA
ART AND ARCHAEOLOGY
THE ART OF ANCIENT PERU
THE ART OF THE ETRUSCANS
THE ART OF ANCIENT MEXICO

Front cover: Jousting armor for man and horse, German, about 1500
The Metropolitan Museum of Art, Rogers Fund, 1904

Back cover: Armor of George Clifford, English, 1590-1595
The Metropolitan Museum of Art, Munsey Fund, 1932

Photographs by Alfred H. Tamarin

 For information address Harper & Row, Publishers, Inc., 10 East 53rd Street, New York, N.Y. 10022. Published simultaneously in Canada by Fitzhenry & Whiteside Limited, Toronto.

Library of Congress Catalog Card Number: 69-10208

Jousting knights, from Tournament Manuscript, German, sixteenth century
The Metropolitan Museum of Art, Rogers Fund, 1922

In Europe during the Middle Ages sons of noble families were trained for knighthood. At the age of seven, boys were sent by their fathers to live in the castles of other noblemen. There they became knights-in-training called *pages.*

The young boys learned the manners of a page: to kneel on one knee before the lord of the castle, to stand as still as a stone unless spoken to, and to bow their heads when answering. They were taught to be courteous and helpful to ladies and to live according to the principles of the Christian religion. Pages also were trained to sing, dance, and play musical instruments.

From *Romance of Alexander,* Flemish, 1338, Bodleian Library, Oxford

In becoming a knight the page was trained to ride a horse, wield a sword, manage a shield, and handle a lance. To perfect his aim with a lance he played *tilting at a quintain.* The quintain was a target fixed to a bar that pivoted on a post. The boy charged at the target with his lance in position. He had to hit the target squarely and move past quickly. If he did not, the bar, which had a sandbag attached, would swing around and hit him.

One of the boys on the left in the illustration above is tilting at a quintain. On the right, another boy is riding a wooden horse pulled by two companions.

The young pages played with marbles and toy knights; they also played ball, walked on stilts, and seesawed.

At the age of fourteen a page became a squire. His chief duties were to help his master into his armor and to keep it polished and repaired. A squire practiced wearing armor to get used to its weight. He became expert at horsemanship and at using a sword and lance. He also groomed the horses and managed the hawks and hounds used for hunting.

Squires' sports were wrestling, fencing, boxing, and swimming. They learned to play chess and backgammon too.

At the right is an illustration of young men training for knighthood.

One of a squire's duties was to stand guard on the walls of the castle. And when a knight rode forth into battle, his squire rode along to serve him, carrying his master's sword, lance, and shield.

Squires were taught the rules of chivalry—a strict code of ethics which knights obeyed—to be religious, honorable, and courteous. Chivalry required that knights be brave, loyal, and just, speak only the truth, be fair to their enemies, help people in distress, protect women, and show mercy to the weak and defenseless.

From Hans Liechtenauer's *Fechtbuch*, German, 1443
The Metropolitan Museum of Art, gift of Miss Marguerite Keasbey, 1926

When a squire performed a deed worthy of knighthood—such as saving his master's life—he was dubbed a knight on the battlefield. His master would tap him on the shoulder with a sword and say, "In the name of God and Saint Michael and Saint George, I dub thee knight. Be brave and loyal."

Usually the squire was dubbed a knight during a long religious service in a castle. First he was given a ritual bath to purify him from sin; then he put on a white tunic. For twenty-four hours before the initiation he had to go without food. He spent all night in the chapel, praying and meditating. His shining new armor, sword, lance, and helmet lay before the altar.

At sunrise he attended church services. Kneeling, the new knight had his sword strapped around his waist, and he took the vows of chivalry. He was tapped on the shoulder with a sword and was told, "Be a good knight." Then his spurs were fastened on, and he received his armor. That evening there was feasting and celebrating. On the right is a painting that shows the ceremony of dubbing a knight.

Detail of "St. Martin Knighted by the Emperor Constantine"
by Bernard van Orley, Flemish, sixteenth century
Nelson Gallery, Atkins Museum, bequest of Henry J. Haskell

Thirteenth-fifteenth century
from *Description du Chateau de Coucy* by Viollet-le-Duc

Life in Europe during the Middle Ages centered about the castle, where a king and his noblemen lived under a system known as *feudalism*. The castle was a fortress which protected the estates called *fiefs*. The land was ruled by the king and by tenants of the king called *vassals*. Many of them had vassals of their own of a lesser rank. A vassal owed military service to his lord. He also supplied military protection to the serfs or peasants who lived and worked on his land.

For protection against attack, a castle was built on a hill or surrounded by a moat, a deep ditch filled with water. The moat could be crossed only by a drawbridge, which could be raised or lowered. The castle was built of stone and had high thick walls.

On top of the walls were battlements from which defenders could shoot arrows down upon attackers. Towers were built at the corners and along the walls so that guards could look out from all sides.

In time of siege the castle had to hold all the fighting knights and their horses, as well as the serfs and enough provisions to last several months.

At the left is a drawing of the Castle of Coucy in France. Below is a photograph of Montebello, a castle in Switzerland, as it looks today. The walls with their notched battlements and the towers can be seen clearly.

Fifteenth century, Swiss National Tourist Office

Thirteenth century, French Government Tourist Office

Whole towns were fortified by building strong walls around them. Carcassonne, a fortified French town of the Middle Ages, was built with a row of double walls for extra protection. Above is a photograph of the city of Carcassonne, which was restored during the nineteenth century.

The illustration at the right shows a fortified town under attack. The defenders are making a *sortie* or counterattack from the gate on the right. An archer is shooting arrows from the battlement, taking careful aim at the enemy. The besiegers have brought up a *trebuchet,* an engine that could hurl round stones at the wall with great force.

Both the attackers and defenders are wearing mail, an early form of armor. Mail was made by linking together thousands of tiny iron rings. It was flexible and strong, and it provided good protection against swords and lances.

The knights are completely covered with mail except for their eyes and noses. They are wearing long cloth surcoats over the mail. Three of the men are carrying shields, each of which bears a decoration identifying its owner.

From an Old Testament manuscript, French, thirteenth century, The Pierpont Morgan Library

Mail was worn by both the English and Norman armies at the Battle of Hastings, which was fought in 1066. In this battle, William, Duke of Normandy, defeated King Harold and conquered England. The story is told in pictures embroidered on a strip of linen 230 feet long known as the Bayeux Tapestry. The section below shows Norman knights on horseback charging English foot soldiers. Both armies are wearing knee-length shirts of mail called *hauberks,* and cone-shaped helmets made of plates of iron, with a metal bar extending over the nose. Both armies are carrying long kite-shaped shields. The Normans are fighting with lances and swords. One of the Englishmen is using a battle-axe, which could crush mail. Armor made of plates of steel was developed as protection against the blows of a battle-axe, war hammer, or mace.

Eleventh century, Bayeux, France, photograph Giraudon

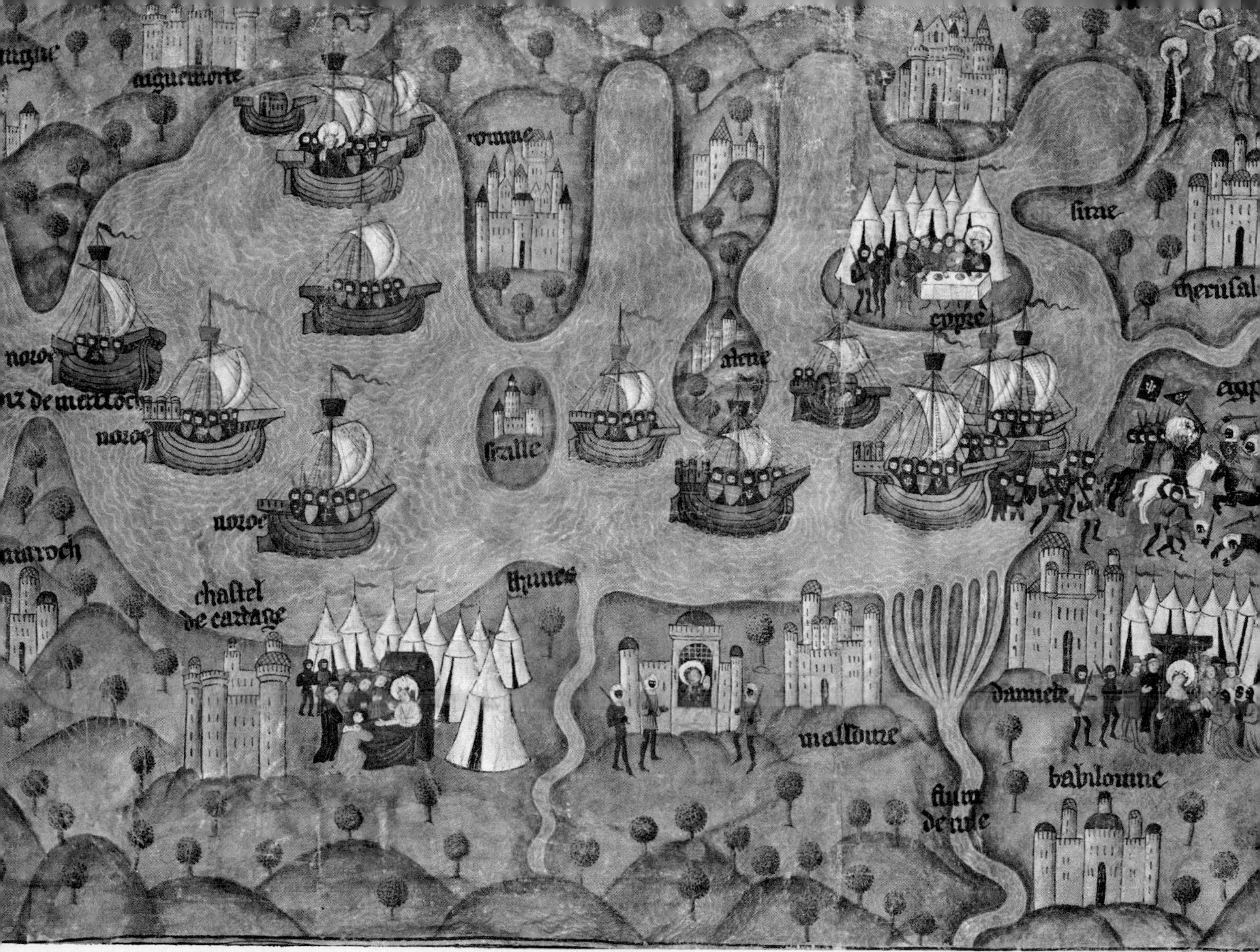

French, fifteenth century, The Metropolitan Museum of Art, gift of J. Pierpont Morgan, 1917

The Crusades were expeditions to the Holy Land to recapture the city of Jerusalem, which had been conquered by the Moslems. There were eight Crusades; they began in the year 1096 and lasted nearly two hundred years.

The seventh and eighth Crusades were led by Louis IX, the French king who became Saint Louis. Above is a map illustrating his two Crusades.

Louis built a port on the Mediterranean Sea called Aigues-Mortes. It is shown in the upper-left corner of the map. The Christian cities are shown with pointed towers. Jerusalem and other Moslem cities are shown with rounded towers. In the lower-right corner is the scene at Damietta in Egypt, where Louis' wife, Margaret, bore him a son. Tunis in North Africa, where Louis died of the plague, is in the lower-left center.

On the two pages that follow is an illustration of Crusaders besieging a city on the coast of the Mediterranean Sea.

OMNIS SPIRITVS

Fifteenth century Bibliothèque Nationale, Paris

The siege of a walled town is shown below. Some attackers are going over the walls on ladders, and others are digging under the walls. The defenders are attempting to beat them off with swords, lances, and boiling oil. The attackers are firing cannons, the earliest guns, first used around the year 1300.

At the right, an army of mounted knights has captured a fortified town. The townspeople are kneeling in surrender on the bridge across the moat. The knights and their horses are wearing heavy armor made of plates of steel.

From *Histoire de Charles Martel,* Flemish, 1468, Bibliothèque Royale, Brussels

By Hans Burgkmair, from *Der Weisskunig*, German, about 1515, The Metropolitan Museum of Art, Dick Fund, 1935

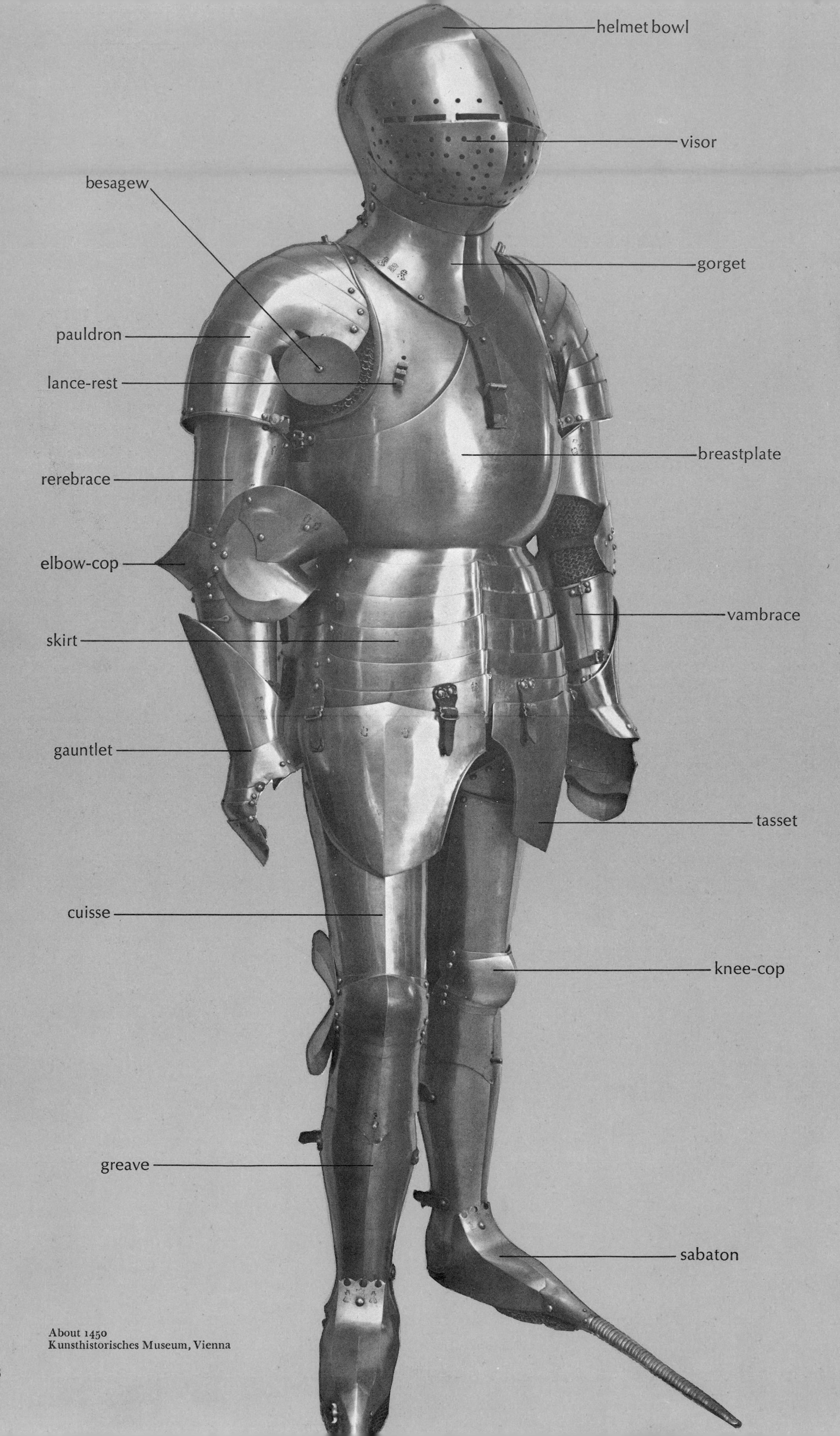

About 1450
Kunsthistorisches Museum, Vienna

A fine suit of armor is a masterpiece of steel sculpture. At the left is a suit of Italian armor showing the names of the important parts. A suit of armor is called a *harness*.

The Italian harness at the right is called a *brigandine,* a style worn by foot soldiers. Brigandine armor is made of narrow scales of steel riveted together and covered with cloth or leather. The jacket of this brigandine is velvet and is lined with sixty-four rows of overlapping steel plates. Mail could be worn underneath for added protection. Brigandines were comfortable, light, and flexible.

The helmet shown here is called a *basinet.* It covers the head completely and has small openings for breathing. The nose is very pointed so that blows will glance off easily.

About 1400
The Metropolitan Museum of Art, Bashford Dean Memorial Collection

A style of armor very popular in the fifteenth century is called *Gothic*. It is slender in form and designed with points and peaks which resemble the pointed and peaked arches and towers of Gothic cathedrals. The surfaces of the German Gothic harness at the left are covered with a pattern of flutings, a series of narrow ridges. These flutings helped deflect weapons from vital spots. Gauntlets, or arm guards, and sabatons, or foot guards, are long and pointed on Gothic armor.

The helmet shown here is a *sallet*, a simple steel hat which once had a padded lining. It has a narrow slit in front through which the knight was able to see.

About 1480
Kunsthistorisches Museum, Vienna

Another style of armor is called *Maximilian.* It was named for Maximilian I, the German emperor who was greatly interested in the manufacture and design of armor. Maximilian armor is rounder and broader than Gothic, and the rows of flutings are vertical and run in parallel lines. The fluting strengthened the metal without adding to its weight. The sabatons on Maximilian armor have broad toes, and the gauntlets have straight edges. The helmet is called a *close helmet.* It has a visor that lifts up to uncover the face.

A harness might weigh sixty pounds or more. Padded cloth garments were worn under the armor for comfort.

German, about 1523
Kunsthistorisches Museum, Vienna

From *Hausbuch der Mendelschen Zwölfbruder*, Stadtbibliothek, Nuremberg

Master armorers of the Middle Ages were important craftsmen. Families handed down their special skills from father to son. Armorers were expert metal workers and could make a harness to the exact measure of the knight who was to wear it. Often a knight would travel far to get a harness that would fit him perfectly.

The armorers studied every muscle and joint of the human body to make armor that would fit the warrior and not hinder his movements. It might take a year or more to make a full suit of armor. The armor had to be strong enough to protect the knight, but at the same time it had to be light enough for him to walk, run, climb a wall, lie down and get up quickly, and mount his horse without help.

Above, an armorer is shown making spurs. At the right is an illustration of an armor workshop. The workers are busily hammering out the different pieces. Finished parts are hanging on the wall—leg defenses, breastplates, helmets, and gauntlets.

By Hans Burgkmair, from *Der Weisskunig*, German, about 1515
The Metropolitan Museum of Art, Dick Fund, 1935

Italian, 1570
The Metropolitan Museum of Art,
Bashford Dean Memorial Collection, 1929

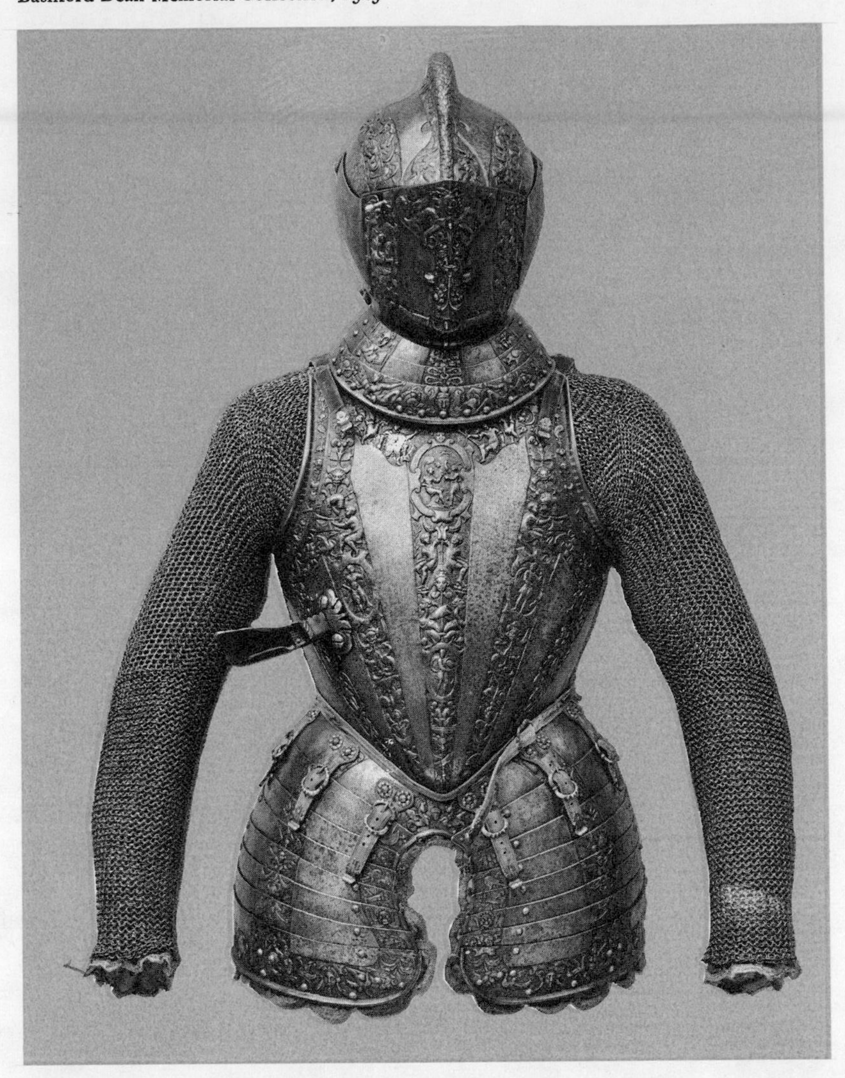

Plate armor was in use from the fourteenth to the eighteenth centuries, and the styles changed greatly during these four hundred years. In later times armor was worn only for ceremonial occasions rather than for protection in battle and was called *parade armor*.

The half-suit above is decorated with elaborate designs which have been embossed or raised in the steel by hammering. Decorated armor was not practical for battle. Embossing stretches metal and weakens it, and the raised designs spoil the smooth glancing surfaces. This suit was made in Milan, Italy, one of the great armor centers of the world.

The parade harness, right, was made in the Royal Armory in Greenwich, England. It belonged to George Clifford, Earl of Cumberland, champion of Queen Elizabeth I.

The harness was *blued* by passing it through a furnace at low heat. Designs were then etched into the surface. Armor to be etched was first painted all over with acidproof varnish. The designs were scratched through the varnish. The armor was then dipped into a bath of acid which ate into the steel where the varnish had been scratched away. The etched designs in George Clifford's armor are gilded.

The Metropolitan Museum of Art, Munsey Fund, 1932

German, fourteenth century
Kunsthistorisches Museum, Vienna

Styles in helmets also changed greatly through the years. Early helmets called *great helms* had flat, round, or cone-shaped tops. The knight was able to see through two narrow slits. The great helm above is decorated with a pair of horns. Great helms were often decorated with crests in the form of birds, animals, banners, or even crowns.

Italian, about 1470
The Metropolitan Museum of Art,
gift of Mrs. George A. Douglass, 1960

Above is a *barbute*, which protects the skull and the sides of the face and neck. It has a T-shaped face opening with a raised border for additional protection.

Below on the left is a *basinet*. It is rounded, and tapers to a point at the top. It has a facelike visor with a long nose and small air holes. A basinet with a long-snouted visor is sometimes called a *pig-faced basinet*. A *camail* or collar of mail was attached to the helmet.

The helmet below on the right is called a *great basinet*. It has a simple, rounded visor with more than 150 openings for seeing and breathing.

German, about 1400
The Metropolitan Museum of Art,
Bashford Dean Memorial Collection, 1929

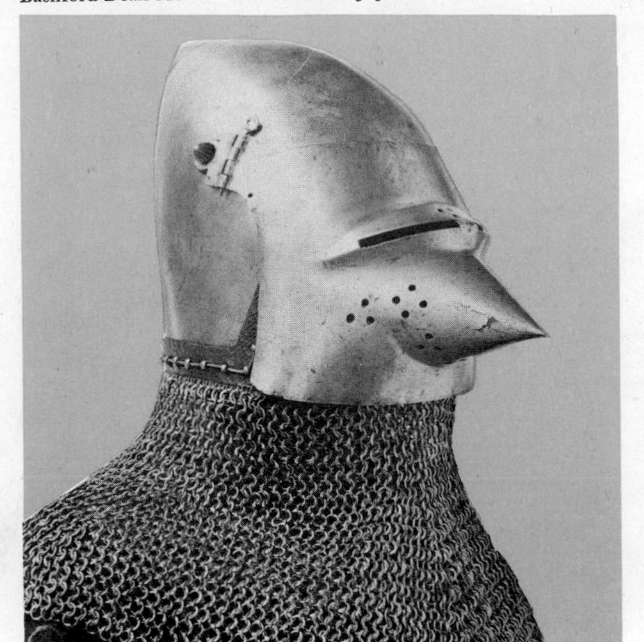

German, about 1450
The Metropolitan Museum of Art, Rogers Fund, 1904

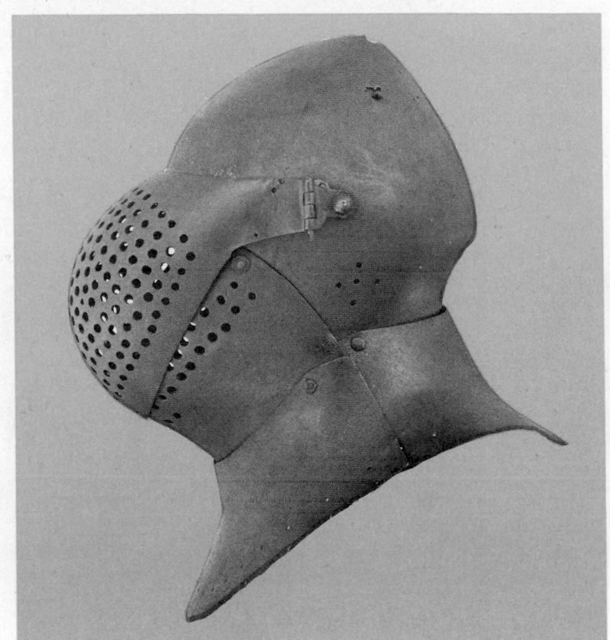

…an, 1570
…e Metropolitan Museum of Art,
gift of W. H. Riggs, 1913

Above is a *morion,* which covers only the head. Archers and musketeers liked morions because it was easier for them to take aim if their faces were not covered.

The parade helmet below has been signed in gold by Philip de Negroli of Milan, a famous Italian armorer. It was hammered out of a single sheet of cold steel, which is difficult to work because it is so hard. Intricate designs were embossed on the helmet, which was probably made for the French King Francis I.

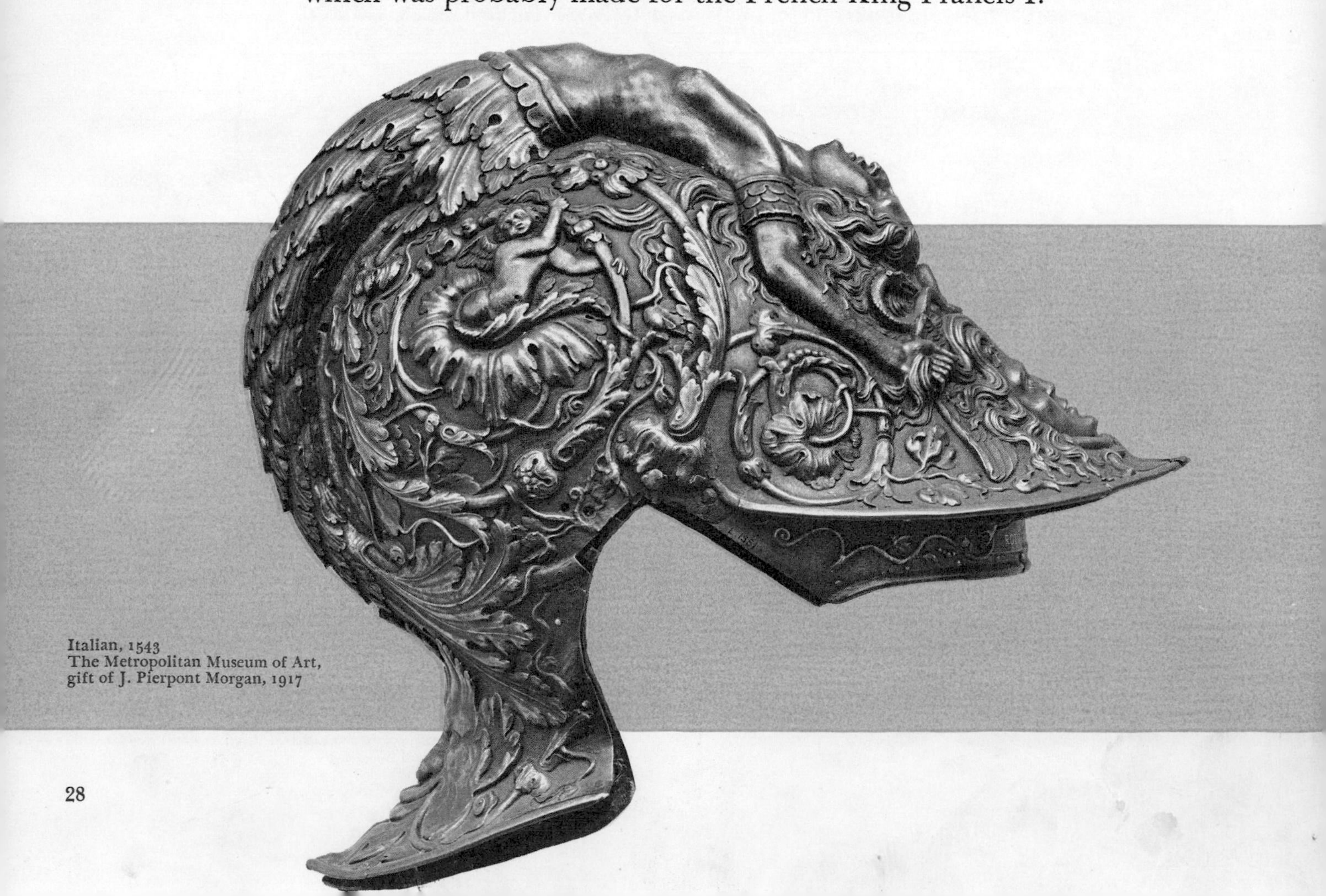

Italian, 1543
The Metropolitan Museum of Art,
gift of J. Pierpont Morgan, 1917

Italian, sixteenth century
The Metropolitan Museum of Art,
gift of W. H. Riggs, 1913

The helmet above is a *burgonet,* a favorite of the infantry, or foot soldiers, and the light cavalry, horsemen who were not fully armored. The burgonet was popular because it is close-fitting and provides enough protection, yet is open enough to allow the wearer to breathe comfortably. The parade helmet below was owned by King Louis XIV of France. It is made of silver, which was blued, and decorated with gilt and bronze. On state occasions it was carried by a page to symbolize Louis' power.

French, about 1700
The Metropolitan Museum of Art,
Rogers Fund, 1904

German, 1548
The Metropolitan Museum of Art,
Rogers Fund, 1932

Armor for horses was developed along with armor for men. Armor for a horse protected mainly the animal's head, neck, and chest. The head covering is called a *chanfron,* and the neck covering is called a *crinet*. The plumes and crests on a knight's helmet identified him.

Spurs were a symbol of knighthood. When a squire was knighted, he was said to have "won his spurs." Spurs were often buried with their owners.

Both examples below with spiked wheels are called *rowel spurs*. Another type has a single spike and is called a *prick spur*.

This elaborate saddle was used for parades and festivals. It is made of wood covered with stag horn, carved with figures of knights, ladies, and dragons.

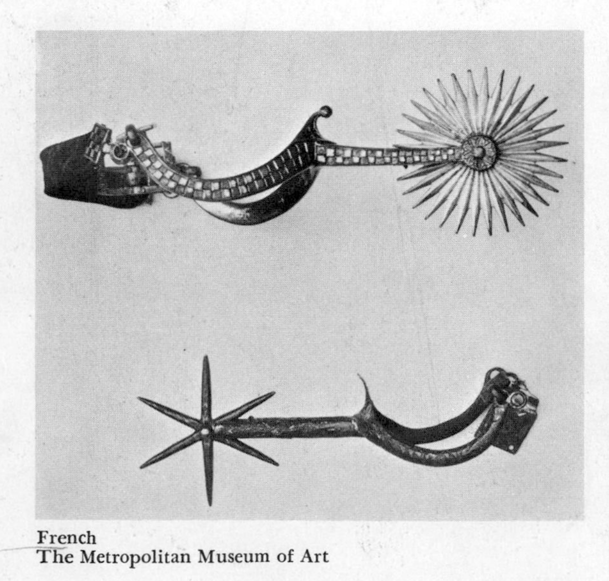

French
The Metropolitan Museum of Art

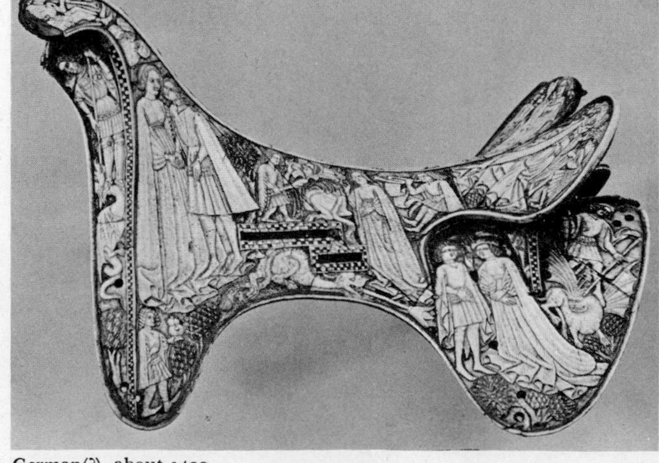

German(?), about 1400
The Metropolitan Museum of Art, Dick Fund, 1940

German, 1515
The Metropolitan Museum of Art, Bashford Dean Memorial Collection

The crossbow was the most important weapon of foot soldiers during the Middle Ages. It was used to shoot short, thick wooden bolts tipped with sharp metal points. The crossbow was so strong that a mechanical winder was needed to pull the cord back and reset it. Crossbows could be carried ready to fire, and they had a long range. In the painting at the left the archer is using a cranequin to draw the bowstring.

The archer below is aiming a crossbow and is ready to press the trigger and release the bolt. Crossbow bolts could pierce all but the heaviest armor, and a well-aimed bolt could hit between the armor joints.

Crossbow bolts were fired at armor in the workshop to test the strength of the metal.

From *Zeugbuch Kaiser Maximilian I*, German, sixteenth century
Kunsthistorisches Museum, Vienna

Detail of "Martyrdom of St. Sebastian" by Hans Holbein the elder, Alte Pinakothek, Munich, about 1515
Bruckmann Art Reference Bureau

Two-handed swords, like the one below, had a straight two-edged blade and an extra-long handle or *hilt.* Specially-trained foot soldiers used them in combat to clear a path for the advancing knights on horseback.

In the illustration below, from the book *The Triumph of Maximilian,* soldiers are carrying two-handed swords.

By Hans Burgkmair, German, 1512–1519
The Metropolitan Museum of Art, Dick Fund, 1932

German, 1610
The Metropolitan Museum of Art, Rogers Fund, 1904

Italian, about 1560
The Wallace Collection, London

A mace, a heavy club used by the cavalry and the infantry, could break through armor. The mace above, decorated with gold and silver, is for ceremonies.

The halberd was a weapon used by foot soldiers. Its point could pierce, and its blade could cut. The hook at the back of the axe blade could be used to drag a knight from his saddle, fell a horse, or scale a wall.

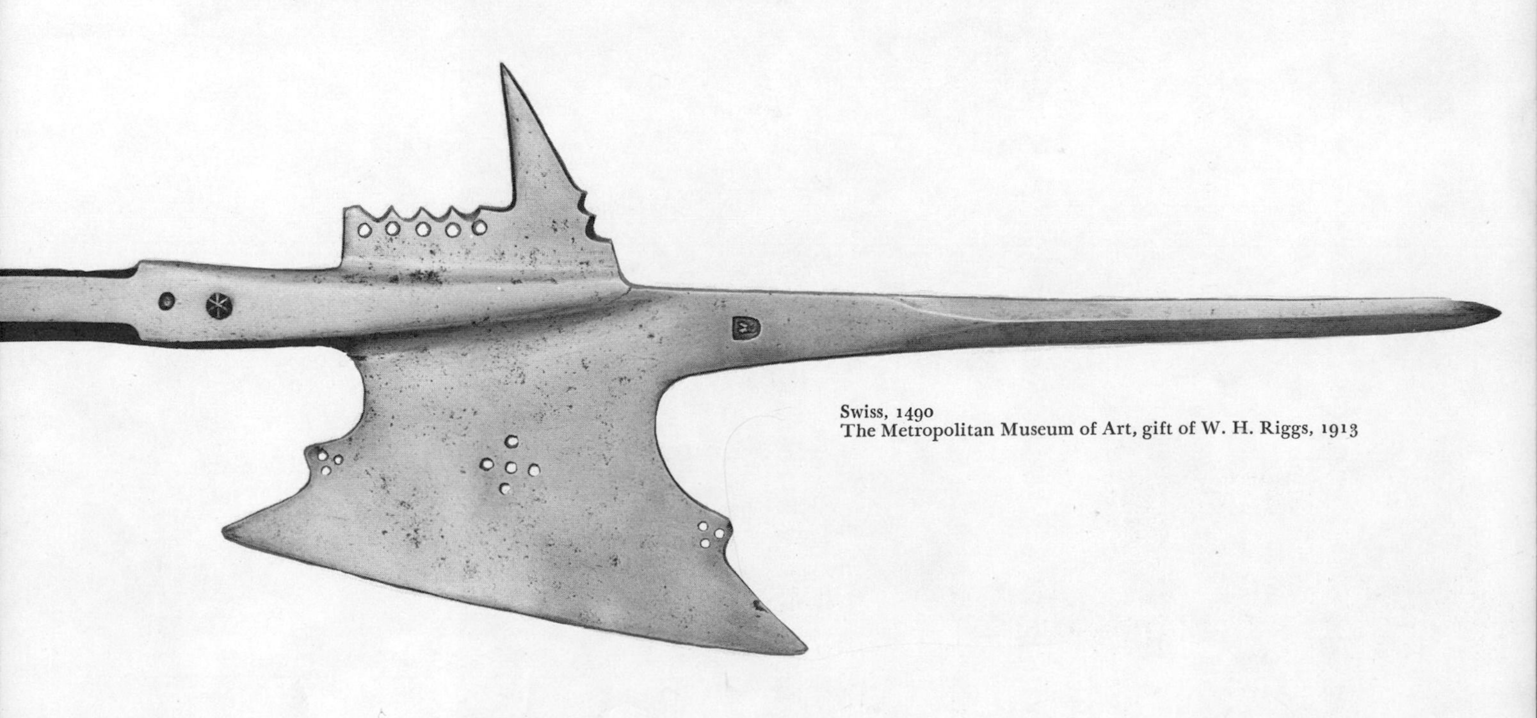

Swiss, 1490
The Metropolitan Museum of Art, gift of W. H. Riggs, 1913

Many legends have been told about the days of knighthood. The best-known are the stories of King Arthur and the Knights of the Round Table. According to these legends, Arthur's knights were the bravest, truest, and boldest knights of all time.

A story tells that when Arthur was born, his father, King Uther Pendragon, put him in the care of the magician Merlin. Arthur was brought up by Merlin and did not know he was the son of a king. When Arthur's father died, a steel anvil appeared atop a great stone in the churchyard. A shining sword was stuck in the anvil. Inscribed in letters of gold were the words "Whoso pulleth out this sword of this stone and anvil is rightwise King born of all England." Many nobles tried, but none could move it. Finally Arthur tried and pulled out the sword with ease. Thus he proved his right to be King.

Arthur's most famous sword was called Excalibur. This sword was a gift from the Lady of the Lake. A story tells that an arm rose out of the water holding Excalibur. Merlin rowed King Arthur out to accept it. When Arthur was dying, he ordered one of his knights to cast the sword back into the lake. A hand rose from the water, caught Excalibur, and vanished.

The tapestry on the left shows Arthur seated on his throne, surrounded by cardinals and bishops.

French, about 1385
The Metropolitan Museum of Art, Cloisters Collection,
Munsey Fund, 1932, and gift of John D. Rockefeller, Jr., 1947

Arthur and his knights held court sitting at a round table so that everyone might have a place of equal honor. Each knight's name was written in letters of gold upon his chair. One chair, known as the "Siege Perilous," remained vacant. It was reserved for the unnamed knight who would be pure of heart and free from sin.

In the illustration below, the empty Siege Perilous has been uncovered and has been inscribed with the name of Galahad. An old man is leading Galahad to take his rightful place between Arthur and Lancelot.

From *Knights of the Holy Grail,* Italian, fourteenth century, Bibliothèque Nationale, Paris

From *Knights of the Holy Grail,* Italian, fourteenth century, Bibliothèque Nationale, Paris

Sir Galahad is the hero of a story about the search for the Holy Grail. It is said that Christ used this chalice at the Last Supper. When Galahad arrived at the Round Table, a vision of the Holy Grail appeared before the knights, then vanished. They all took a vow to search for it. Galahad in his quest for the Grail found a shield which God had provided for him. It had been awaiting him for centuries behind an altar in an abbey. This shield was as white as snow and had a red cross in the middle.

Later Galahad heard a voice telling him to go to the Castle of the Maidens, where seven wicked brothers held a duke's daughters and their ladies prisoners. Galahad overcame the seven knights single-handedly. Above is an illustration showing Galahad doing battle with three of the brothers. On the right stands an old man clutching the key to the castle. Behind him are the rescued maidens.

The greatest knight of the Round Table was Lancelot, who was said to be Galahad's father. As a child Lancelot had been carried off by the Lady of the Lake and was brought up by her. Lancelot was knighted by King Arthur and later became the champion of Arthur's wife, Queen Guinevere.

When Queen Guinevere was kidnapped by a prince and imprisoned in his father's castle, Lancelot went forth to rescue her. He came upon a swift, raging river. The bridge across it was a polished, gleaming sword, with two lions guarding its farther end.

From *Lancelot-du-Lac,* French, fourteenth century, The Pierpont Morgan Library

Above, Lancelot is shown crossing the bridge, gripping it with bleeding hands and feet. His shield, decorated with red bands, is strapped to his back. Queen Guinevere and the king are looking down from the tower. In the next scene, at the right of the tower, Lancelot approaches them.

Lancelot became so famous that his very name or the sight of his shield frightened his opponents, and they would refuse to fight him. Therefore, he often fought in disguise, using a plain or borrowed shield as shown below.

Above, King Arthur is shown watching a tournament at Camelot, surrounded by the ladies of the court. A tournament was a mock battle between two groups of knights, and a joust was a contest between individual knights. These contests kept knights in training during times of peace. They were tests of strength and skillful horsemanship. They were also magnificent

From a prose romance of Tristan, French, 1463, Bibliothèque Nationale, Paris

social occasions. Kings and their knights wore rich armor, embroidered materials, and jeweled crowns.

Women usually presented the prizes at tournaments, and often a knight carried a favor from his ladylove—a glove, handkerchief, or veil. Trumpets blared at the start of the event and feasts and dancing followed it.

From Codex Manesse, German, fourteenth century, The University of Heidelberg Library

There were many different types of jousts, each with its own elaborate rules and scoring systems. Often a knight used blunted weapons and tried to knock an opponent off his horse.

Efforts were made to prevent serious injury; yet knights were often hurt. Above, a contestant falls from his horse, his helmet pierced by a shattered lance. The ladies of the court are distressed.

As a safety measure the tilt was developed, a barrier separating the two horses so that they would not collide. Tilt became the word used for the joust itself.

The illustration below shows the gorgeous pageantry of a joust. The horses are richly decked in colorful cloth. Squires on horseback hold extra lances. The knights wear elaborate jousting armor, with decorative crests on their helmets to identify them. A white veil, probably a lady's favor, hangs from the helmet of the knight in the foreground. The three tents are pavilions where the knights put on their armor.

From Jean Froissart's Chronicle, French, fifteenth century, The British Museum

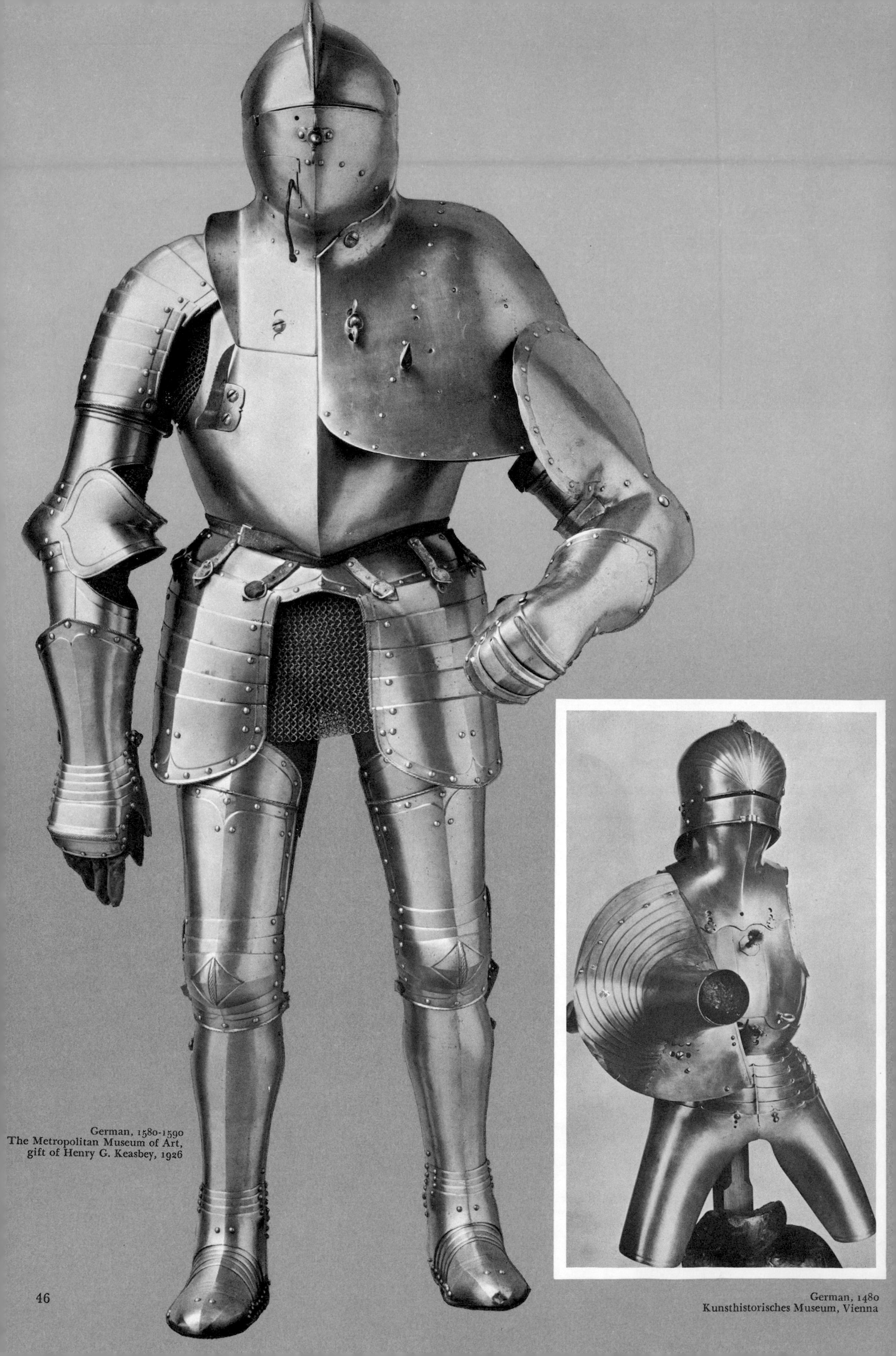

German, 1580-1590
The Metropolitan Museum of Art,
gift of Henry G. Keasbey, 1926

German, 1480
Kunsthistorisches Museum, Vienna

At first, armor used for jousting was the same as the armor worn in battle. Then heavier and thicker armor was developed for tilting. Heavier helmets could be used in a joust because they were worn for such a short time. Some helmets weighed more than twenty pounds. Often a jousting helmet was bolted to a breastplate. Sometimes an extra capelike protection called a *grandguard* was added to the left shoulder. A hook was attached to the right side of the chest to help the knight balance and thrust his lance.

In tournaments fought with sharp lances, a large circular plate called a *vamplate* was used to protect the right hand and arm. A lance protruded through the center of the vamplate.

Sometimes trials by combat were fought and deadly weapons were used. People believed that God would see that justice was done and that a knight's guilt or innocence was proved by his success or defeat in combat.

German, 1545
The Metropolitan Museum of Art,
gift of W. H. Riggs, 1913

Ornament of horse trappings,
About 1300
The Metropolitan Museum of Art,
Rogers Fund, 1904

As gunpowder changed the nature of warfare, knights in armor lost their usefulness. But knights and knighthood did not entirely disappear. In Europe today men are still dubbed knights for outstanding achievements or courageous deeds. Among the best-known orders of chivalry still in existence are the Order of the Garter in England, the Order of the Golden Fleece in Spain, and the Maltese Knights.

We can see armor in museums today because it was preserved through the ages. It had been hung in churches where the knights were buried. Other harnesses stood in the halls of castles and great homes, handed down in noble families from generation to generation.

The code of chivalry is still the guide for gentlemanly behavior. And the rules of the tournament set up a standard of good sportsmanship which still affects our games.